A

SHEFFIELD

LASS

By

Pamela Griffiths

I was born Pamela (Nee) Cocker in Sheffield, 27th September 1952; my parents Dorothy (Nee) Lee and Derek Cocker were both born in Sheffield.

I am the widow of Clive Griffiths, I have three children, a stepson and nine grandchildren. I have a diploma in freelance journalism, a diploma in quality management. I am retired from working for the NHS in Development and Quality Management. I live in Loxley Valley, Sheffield with my partner Sandy Hoffman.

I won the National Local Poem competition 2011 with 'Home Sweet Home in Loxley Valley'. The presentation was in the Sheffield Central Library and appeared in the Sheffield Star/Telegraph newspapers and on a video on their website. I've been published in over sixty poetry anthologies. I have also been included in Poets of the Year books, diaries and on CD's. My own poetry books include 'Expressions of Life', 'Moments in Time', 'Life is a Spiral Staircase' and 'A Sheffield Lass'.

'The Stamp Master' is my first novel in the DCI Chrissie Charles detective thriller books and is now available in paperback and kindle format on amazon.

Website – www.pamelagriffiths.com

Twitter - @pamg56

Facebook – Author Pamela Griffiths

A CIP catalogue record for this book is available from the British Library.

ISBN 978-0-85781-546-0

CLASSIFICATION: POETRY

First published in Great Britain in 2015

By

United Press Ltd,

London.

2nd edition re-published 2015

CONTENTS

A Bus Ride Away

A Girls Night In

A New Life

A Sheffield Lass

Another Year Bites The Dust

Born In The Fifties

Childhood

Crossroads

Gone But Never Forgotten

How It Was In The Past

Life Is Like A Time Bomb

Living In Sheffield

Living The I-Life

Nothing Is The Same

One Day

What Happens Next?

A Bus Ride Away

We are all guilty of letting things slide
All for the sake of a short bus ride
It doesn't matter if it's near or far
We could go by taxi or drive in the car

Your friends and family are waiting for you
You haven't got the time no matter what you do
It's a shame but its true time moves on
Before too long many years have gone

Putting things off I haven't got the time
If it isn't entered into this diary of mine
Procrastination is a common failing
And because life isn't always plain sailing

Intentions are good but never ideal
I try to ignore the guilt I now feel
It really wasn't meant to be this way
After all it's only a bus ride away

A Girls Night In

It had been a while since we all last met
We have all matured with grace
So our girls night in was special for us
We just hoped we could take the pace

We had a few drinks and had a laugh
And acted so immature
But it wouldn't be us if we didn't do that
For our silliness there isn't a cure

We were reminiscing of years gone by
Howling like wolves we joked and laughed
We were giggling like a group of hens
We golden girls love acting daft

As the night went on the drinks flowed freely
We tried not to spill a drop
The time passed quickly the hours just flew
But we didn't want the laughter to stop

We have decided we should do it again
We had all enjoyed a great night
A girls night in is a wonderful thing
But we must have looked quite a sight

A New life

Everyone is born without prejudice or sin
When a baby is born a new life will begin
What happens after that depends on indoctrination
The miracle of life is part of our creation

Innocence is special it doesn't last long
Soon a child grows into where it will belong
After a few years the child will be told
What it should be, then the child will unfold

Some children are born into a life that's sound
It is always good to have both parents around
Teaching children, it's hard to make them see
You have to work hard you don't get anything free

If mistakes are made it isn't too late
Learn from them to make life great
A child grows up as the parents then choose
Don't let them rule then you've nothing to lose

They will grow and mature to be part of you
They will always remind you of what you used to do
Children are born as a blank page in time
They grow so fast but will they tow the line?

The first few years determine who we are
There isn't any shortcut we can see that from afar
When a child is born a brand new life has begun
Children are the future generations to come

A Sheffield Lass

I was born and bred in Sheffield
Back in an era of old
I lived throughout a time
When old wife's tales were still told

My childhood in the fifties
Was full of love and fun
Our elders we respected
As for poverty there was some

Smoke from the steel works bellowed
Smog would pollute the air
Coal was burnt to warm us
But the smoke was everywhere

Houses were small and cramped
Cold and damp they were
Now we all have bathrooms
I know which I prefer

In those years of childhood
I was taught right from wrong
In Sheffield I grew to adulthood
It's my home it's where I belong

Old and dirty steel works
Were shutting one by one
Many were made redundant
Their livelihood now gone

As a city we all battled through
To put us back on track
New industries and houses were built
Now there was no going back

Throughout my life in Sheffield
I was proud to live it here
Things have changed so much
Not all for the better I fear

We can't hold back the hands of time
Everything moves on
As technology takes over
My past history has now gone

Proud to be part of Sheffield
Brought up with the working class
I am getting old and retired now
But I'm still that Sheffield lass

ANOTHER YEAR BITES THE DUST

As another year bites the dust
A new one takes it's place
This is how the lifespan works
In the human race

I'll take the bull by the horns
I've got nothing to lose
Lots of new options now
There are plenty I could choose

No regrets have I
Nothing is that bad
I've had a good life
Even though some was sad

Life is what you make of it
It's mind over matter
Let the cogs turn around
With minimal clatter

It's time to toast the future
Here's to another new year
Hoping for a good one
As the bells ring loud and clear

BORN IN THE FIFTIES

My earliest memories
As I recall
Is hearing the
Big drop hammers fall

I was just a child
Laying in my cot
Those special memories
I never forgot

I was born in the fifties
I was on the ball
I was very advanced
As I now recall

The dark held for me
Deep and dark fears
The drop hammer left me
With ringing in my ears

I stood up in my cot
A defenceless child
In my mind I collected
All those thoughts I filed

We had a black and white TV
The envy of our street
We were working class people
The best you'd ever meet

Money, we never had much
But that never made things bad
We were brought up to be grateful
For everything that we had

Life was so much simpler then
We all did what we had to do
We all mucked in together
As the road to adulthood grew

As I look back it's sad
To think all that has gone
This lifestyle won't return again
Because things always move on

Back in the fifties
It was good in that era
A long road ahead
Getting nearer and nearer

CHILDHOOD

We made our own amusement
We didn't have many toys
It was fun playing hide and seek
Playing kiss catch with the boys

If it was fine we would play outside
We could always find something to do
At the little shop on the corner
We would buy a penny chew

We played at hop scotch for hours
Drawing squares with chalk on the path
The hours went by so quickly
Soon it was time for our tea and a bath

We were taught to never be cheeky
And not to answer back
If when we rarely misbehaved
We would certainly get a smack

I grew up with values
It created who I am
So now that I have retired
Just call me poet Pam

CROSSROADS

I am standing at the crossroads
From four paths I have to choose
If I choose the wrong one
There is so much that I'll lose

One path leads to the deepest sea
If I follow it I might drown
One path leads to the heavenly stars
If I follow this I'll shine down

Another path takes me to the sun
If I follow it I'll crash and burn
I need to choose the right path
I know that I cannot return

One path will take me to safety
So I silently say a prayer
The path I follow once chosen
Will lead me to who knows where

I don't have much time left
To choose the path I must take
I walk along my chosen path
Then suddenly I'm wide awake

The crossroads they were just a dream
Hiding in my subconscious mind
In my dream I had made a decision
While awake the path I will find

Choices have to be made
Impacting on life all the time
If I make the wrong decisions
It could ruin this life of mine

So as I approach my crossroads
Wondering which path I should take
The tides of time are watching me
To see if I make a mistake

GONE BUT NEVER FORGOTTEN

People are born and then they die
This is just part of life's plan
We live our lives how we want
And do whatever we can

When a loved one dies it hurts us
There is nothing we can do
They are gone but never forgotten
Relatively life just flew

We have all lost someone special
Parents, siblings, friends and pets
They are gone but never forgotten
That is as good as it gets

Sadness surrounds bereavement
Looking back on better days
They're gone but never forgotten
Remembered in so many ways

Life is precious and blessed
We all deserve one more chance
We hope we will not be forgotten
As we dance our very last dance

Faith, hope and forgiveness
Helping others is what we do
Those who've gone, will not be forgotten
One day it will be me and you

We enter this world with nothing
We go out with nothing too
There isn't much point in collecting
You can't take anything but you

Loved ones sadly pass away
We try not to dwell on it though
They are gone but never forgotten
In the end we all have to go

It's sad when we look back
To happier times now gone
They are gone but never forgotten
It's time for us to move on

HOW IT WAS IN THE PAST

Time goes along
Just ticking away
We hope our dreams
Are here to stay

Living in the present
Following the past
Knowing that life
Will never last

Sometimes looking back
To the good old days
It was easier then
In so many ways

Changes are inevitable
As times move on
As it was in the past
Those days have gone

I loved bread and dripping
That was so good
I'd eat it now
If only I could

Homemade cooking
Was such a treat
All made from scratch
Was so good to eat

As technology improves
It's not the same
It is brilliant in some ways
In others it's a shame

In this digital age
Things move on so fast
Sometimes I look back
To how it was in the past

LIFE IS LIKE A TIME BOMB

Life is like a time bomb
Waiting to explode
Ticking away as we follow
The ever twisting road

Life is like a time bomb
Waiting in the wings
What we gain on the roundabout
We lose on the swings

Life is like a time bomb
It couldn't care less
We could be very happy
Or be suffering from stress

Life is like a time bomb
As we swallow life's pill
If one thing doesn't get us
Then something else will

Life is like a time bomb
Ticking merrily away
Soon it will catch up with us
And blow us all away

LIVING IN SHEFFIELD

I have always loved living in Sheffield
I have lived here all my life
From being a child I loved it
Then grew up as a mother and wife

I have seen many changes
Throughout my sixty plus years
Some were for the better
But some brought saddened tears

The buses and trams then were common
With the old open plan entry
They were full of coughing smokers
And smokers back then there were plenty

When I was at school it was daunting
We treated our elders with respect
Manners were instilled into us
Those we were never allowed to neglect

We had to work had from being young
But we also played hard too
I remember the old Buccaneer pub
Done up like a ship don't you?

Pubs, shops and clubs have come and gone
The hole in the road has gone too
These were all features throughout my life
Changed now but what can you do?

There were lots of cinemas in Sheffield
They all had ashtrays inside
It was the highlight of the week
A place for young couples to hide

LIVING THE I-LIFE

Oh how things have changed
Technology has moved us on
In a very short life span
All the good eras have gone

What would we do without iPhones?
We would feel cut off
There is even an i-linctus
That detects and cures any cough

I-toothpaste can detect
What your dental needs are
Computers can control our lives
Even when driving the car

The iPhone, iPad and iCloud
Have all become part of our i-plan
In this world of the i-life
We will always say i-can

We can work and stay in i-touch
We can tweet on Twitter too
We are all living the i-life
It controls everything that we do

NOTHING IS THE SAME

I'm now sixty two, a bit long in the tooth
But I can still remember, my years as a youth
Young and free, not a care in the world
I straightened my hair, as it naturally curled

I applied my make up, thick and black
It was the fashion then, I kept on track
Back in the day, the trains spewed out steam
No digital TV's were there to be seen

People worked very hard back then
They helped each other as and when
Late at night, steel works were alive
On molten metal, drop hammers would dive

The factories diminished, over the years
Many lost their jobs and had to change careers
Nothing is the same, times have changed
I'm not sure I like how it's all been rearranged

ONE DAY

One day in my life is a portion
A little cog in a giant wheel
Even though just a drop in the ocean
Its ok this day is for real

This day maybe insignificant now
But in the whole scale of things
Today isn't meant to mean anything
Just whatever this day brings

Whether or not it is happy
It is still an important day
This time is now and forever
And it can't be taken away

One day goes before and after
Another day passes again
Sometimes it is full of passion
Another is full of pain

As I reflect back on this day
I know it is all down to me
Whatever happens on this day
Whatever will be will be

So many days went before this
Many days will pass once it's gone
This is one day in a lifetime
And life goes on and on

WHAT HAPPENS NEXT?

What happens next when you've done everything?
When that era is done what will life bring?
Life has a habit of turning things around
When one door closes another is found

Is there a scope to achieve much more?
What lies behind that new open door?
From one era to another a transition is made
Old achievements are gone new plans are now laid

Time washes away and cleanses my soul
Cleanliness follows as I find a new goal
Wizened and wrinkled from corrosion of time
My life is predestined the outlook seems fine

So even though this chapter is finished
The outcome for me has not diminished
What happens next? That all depends
A means to an end on what fate now sends

A Sheffield Lass – ISBN 978-0-85781-546-0

A Sheffield Lass is the fourth book of Pamela's poetry, they were first published by United Press Ltd. London.

Other books by Pamela Griffiths include:

Expressions of Life – Poetry
Moments in time – Poetry
Life is a Spiral Staircase – Poetry

The Stamp Master – Detective Thriller book one in the DCI Chrissie Charles novels

Check out all her many books on amazon.co.uk or on Facebook or Twitter.

A big thank you to all my readers for purchasing this book.

Thank you for supporting and encouraging me to continue writing, it means a great deal to me.

Pamela Griffiths

www.ingramcontent.com/pod-product-compliance
Lightning Source LLC
Chambersburg PA
CBHW061107050726
47592CB00004B/1867